TENOR SAX

HAL•LEONARD
INSTRUMENTAL
PLAY-ALONG

AUDIO
ACCESS
INCLUDED

PLAYBACK+
Speed • Pitch • Balance • Loop

HIP-HOP HITS

T0057852

Audio arrangements by Peter Deneff

To access audio, visit:
www.halleonard.com/mylibrary

Enter Code
2825-3943-0095-8816

ISBN 978-1-5400-8261-9

HAL•LEONARD®

For all works contained herein:
Unauthorized copying, arranging, adapting, recording, Internet posting, public performance,
or other distribution of the music in this publication is an infringement of copyright.
Infringers are liable under the law.

Visit Hal Leonard Online at
www.halleonard.com

Contact us:
Hal Leonard
7777 West Bluemound Road
Milwaukee, WI 53213
Email: info@halleonard.com

In Europe, contact:
Hal Leonard Europe Limited
42 Wigmore Street
Marylebone, London, W1U 2RN
Email: info@halleonardeurope.com

In Australia, contact:
Hal Leonard Australia Pty. Ltd.
4 Lentara Court
Cheltenham, Victoria, 3192 Australia
Email: info@halleonard.com.au

CONTENTS

BANG BANG
(Rap Version)

TENOR SAX

Words and Music by ONIKA MARAJ,
MAX MARTIN, SAVAN KOTECHA
and RICKARD GÖRANSSON

Copyright © 2014 MONEY MACK MUSIC, HARAJUKU BARBIE MUSIC, MXM MUSIC AB and BMG GOLD SONGS
All Rights for MONEY MACK MUSIC and HARAJUKU BARBIE MUSIC Administered by SONGS OF UNIVERSAL, INC.
All Rights for MXM MUSIC AB Administered by KOBALT SONGS MUSIC PUBLISHING
All Rights for BMG GOLD SONGS Administered by BMG RIGHTS MANAGEMENT (US) LLC
All Rights Reserved   Used by Permission

TALK

TENOR SAX

Words and Music by KHALID ROBINSON,
GUY LAWRENCE and HOWARD LAWRENCE

Copyright © 2019 Sony/ATV Music Publishing LLC and Universal Music Publishing Ltd.
All Rights on behalf of Sony/ATV Music Publishing LLC Administered by Sony/ATV Music Publishing LLC, 424 Church Street, Suite 1200, Nashville, TN 37219
All Rights on behalf of Universal Music Publishing Ltd. Administered by Universal - PolyGram International Tunes, Inc.
International Copyright Secured   All Rights Reserved

GOODBYES

TENOR SAX

Words and Music by AUSTIN POST,
BRIAN LEE, LOUIS BELL,
WILLIAM WALSH, JEFFREY LAMAR WILLIAMS,
VAL BLAVATNIK and JESSIE LAUREN FOUTZ

Copyright © 2019 SONGS OF UNIVERSAL, INC., POSTY PUBLISHING, DONG HOE MUSIC, EMI APRIL MUSIC INC., NYANKINGMUSIC,
WMMW PUBLISHING, RESERVOIR 416, YOUNG STONER LIFE PUBLISHING, WARNER-TAMERLANE PUBLISHING CORP.,
VALENTIN BLAVATNIK PUB DESIGNEE and JESSIE LAUREN FOUTZ PUBLISHING DESIGNEE
All Rights for POSTY PUBLISHING and DONG HOE MUSIC Administered by SONGS OF UNIVERSAL, INC.
All Rights for EMI APRIL MUSIC INC., NYANKINGMUSIC and WMMW PUBLISHING Administered by
SONY/ATV MUSIC PUBLISHING LLC, 424 Church Street, Suite 1200, Nashville, TN 37219
All Rights for RESERVOIR 416 and YOUNG STONER LIFE PUBLISHING Administered Worldwide by RESERVOIR MEDIA MANAGEMENT, INC.
All Rights for VALENTIN BLAVATNIK PUB DESIGNEE Administered by WARNER-TAMERLANE PUBLISHING CORP.
All Rights Reserved   Used by Permission

HOLD UP

TENOR SAX

Words and Music by BEYONCÉ KNOWLES,
UZOECHI EMENIKE, DEANDRE WAY, DOC POMUS,
MORT SHUMAN, SEAN RHODEN, KAREN ORZOLEK,
NICHOLAS ZINNER, BRIAN CHASE, KELVIN McCONNELL,
ANTONIO RANDOLPH, EMILE HAYNIE, THOMAS PENTZ,
JOSHUA TILLMAN and EZRA KOENIG

© 2016 WARNER CHAPPELL MUSIC LTC., SOULJA BOY TELLEM MUSIC, WC MUSIC CORP., OAKLAND 13 MUSIC, BEYONCE PUBLISHING,
UNICHAPPELL MUSIC INC., MORT SHUMAN SONGS, 456 MUSIC ASSOCIATES, BMG PLATINUM SONGS US, MELOXTRA PUBLISHING,
BMG RIGHTS MANAGEMENT (UK) LIMITED, EMI BLACKWOOD MUSIC INC., DISASTER PUBLISHING, BIG-N-MAGE PUBLISHING, UNIVERSAL MUSIC CORP.,
HEAVYCRATE PUBLISHING, KMR MUSIC ROYALTIES II SCSP, SUGAR POP MEOW MEOW and EZRA KOENIG PUBLISHING DESIGNEE
All Rights for OAKLAND 13 MUSIC and BEYONCE PUBLISHING Administered by WC MUSIC CORP.
All Rights for MORT SHUMAN SONGS and 456 MUSIC ASSOCIATES Administered by UNICHAPPELL MUSIC INC.
All Rights for BMG PLATINUM SONGS US, MELOXTRA PUBLISHING and BMG RIGHTS MANAGEMENT (UK) LIMITED
Administered by BMG RIGHTS MANAGEMENT (US) LLC
All Rights for EMI BLACKWOOD MUSIC INC., DISASTER PUBLISHING and BIG-N-MAGE PUBLISHING
Administered by SONY/ATV MUSIC PUBLISHING LLC, 424 Church Street, Suite 1200, Nashville, TN 37219
All Rights for HEAVYCRATE PUBLISHING Administered by UNIVERSAL MUSIC CORP.
All Rights for KMR MUSIC ROYALITES II SCSP and SUGAR POP MEOW MEOW Administered Worldwide by KOBALT SONGS MUSIC PUBLISHING
All Rights Reserved   Used by Permission
- Contains samples of "Can't Get Used To Losing You" by Doc Pomus and Mort Shuman, © 1963 (Renewed) 456 Music Associates and Unichappell Music Inc.

JUICE

TENOR SAX

Words and Music by LIZZO,
THERON MAKIEL THOMAS, ERIC FREDERIC,
SAM SUMSER and SEAN SMALL

© 2019 WARNER-TAMERLANE PUBLISHING CORP., MELISSA JEFFERSON PUBLISHING DESIGNEE,
T N T EXPLOSIVE PUBLISHING, SONY/ATV MUSIC PUBLISHING LLC, SONGS FROM THE BOARDWALK, FREDERIC AND RIED MUSIC,
RESERVOIR 416, WIKISONGZ and SEAN SMALL PUBLISHING DESIGNEE
All Rights for MELISSA JEFFERSON PUBLISHING DESIGNEE Administered by WARNER-TAMERLANE PUBLISHING CORP.
All Rights for T N T EXPLOSIVE PUBLISHING Administered by BMG RIGHTS MANAGEMENT (US) LLC
All Rights for SONY/ATV MUSIC PUBLISHING LLC, SONGS FROM THE BOARDWALK and FREDERIC AND RIED MUSIC
Administered by SONY/ATV MUSIC PUBLISHING LLC, 424 Church Street, Suite 1200, Nashville, TN 37219
All Rights for RESERVOIR 416 and WIKISONGZ Administered Worldwide by RESERVOIR MEDIA MANAGEMENT, INC.
All Rights Reserved   Used by Permission

To Coda ⊕

D.S. al Coda

CODA ⊕

LET YOU DOWN

TENOR SAX

Words and Music by TOMMEE PROFITT
and NATE FEUERSTEIN

© 2017 TOMMEE PROFITT SONGS (ASCAP), NF REAL PUBLISHING (BMI), CAPITOL CMG GENESIS (ASCAP) and CAPITOL CMG PARAGON (BMI)
Admin. at CAPITOLCMGPUBLISHING.COM
All Rights Reserved   Used by Permission

LUCID DREAMS

TENOR SAX

Words and Music by JARAD HIGGINS,
DOMINIC MILLER, GORDON SUMNER,
DANNY SNODGRASS JR. and NICHOLAS MIRA

Copyright © 2018 BMG Platinum Songs, EMI Blackwood Music Inc., Magnetic Publishing Ltd., Steerpike Ltd., EMI Music Publishing Ltd.,
Taz Taylor Beats, Artist 101 Publishing Group, Songs Of Universal, Inc., Electric Feel Music and Nick Mira Publishing
All Rights for BMG Platinum Songs Administered by BMG Rights Management (US) LLC
All Rights for EMI Blackwood Music Inc., Magnetic Publishing Ltd., Steerpike Ltd. and EMI Music Publishing Ltd. Administered by
Sony/ATV Music Publishing LLC, 424 Church Street, Suite 1200, Nashville, TN 37219
All Rights for Taz Taylor Beats and Artist 101 Publishing Group Administered Worldwide by Songs Of Kobalt Music Publishing
All Rights for Electric Feel Music and Nick Mira Publishing Administered by Songs Of Universal, Inc.
International Copyright Secured   All Rights Reserved

OLD TOWN ROAD
(Remix)

TENOR SAX

Words and Music by TRENT REZNOR,
BILLY RAY CYRUS, JOCELYN DONALD,
ATTICUS ROSS, KIOWA ROUKEMA
and MONTERO LAMAR HILL

Copyright © 2019 Form And Texture, Inc., Sunnageronimo Publishing Inc., Songs By MPA,
Songs Of Universal, Inc., Songs In The Key Of Mink and Sony/ATV Music Publishing LLC
All Rights for Form And Texture, Inc., Sunnageronimo Publishing Inc. and Songs By MPA Administered Worldwide by Kobalt Songs Music Publishing
All Rights for Songs In The Key Of Mink Administered by Songs Of Universal, Inc.
All Rights for Sony/ATV Music Publishing LLC Administered by Sony/ATV Music Publishing LLC, 424 Church Street, Suite 1200, Nashville, TN 37219
All Rights Reserved   Used by Permission
- Incorporates the song "34 Ghosts IV" (Words and Music by Atticus Ross and Trent Reznor)

SUCKER FOR PAIN

TENOR SAX

Words and Music by ALEX GRANT, WAYNE SERMON,
DANIEL REYNOLDS, BENJAMIN McKEE, DANIEL PLATZMAN,
DWAYNE CARTER, ROBERT HALL, CAMERON THOMAZ,
TYRONE WILLIAMS GRIFFIN JR. and SAM HARRIS

Copyright © 2017 SONGS OF UNIVERSAL, INC., KIDINAKORNER2 PUBLISHING, SONGS FOR KIDINAKORNER, IMAGINE DRAGONS PUBLISHING,
WARNER-TAMERLANE PUBLISHING CORP., WIZ KHALIFA PUBLISHING, YOUNG MONEY PUBLISHING, INC., THREE OH ONE PRODUCTIONS,
EMI BLACKWOOD MUSIC INC., ITS DRUGS PUBLISHING, S NELSON HARRIS PUBLISHING and KMR MUSIC ROYALTIES II SCSP
All Rights for KIDINAKORNER2 PUBLISHING, SONGS FOR KIDINAKORNER and IMAGINE DRAGONS PUBLISHING Administered by SONGS OF UNIVERSAL, INC.
All Rights for WIZ KHALIFA PUBLISHING, YOUNG MONEY PUBLISHING, INC. and THREE OH ONE PRODUCTIONS
Administered by WARNER-TAMERLANE PUBLISHING CORP.
All Rights for EMI BLACKWOOD MUSIC INC. and ITS DRUGS PUBLISHING
Administered by SONY/ATV MUSIC PUBLISHING LLC, 424 Church Street, Suite 1200, Nashville, TN 37219
All Rights for S NELSON HARRIS PUBLISHING and KMR MUSIC ROYALTIES II SCSP Administered Worldwide by SONGS OF KOBALT MUSIC PUBLISHING
All Rights Reserved   Used by Permission

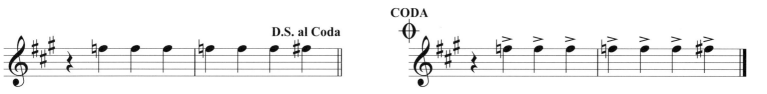

SUNFLOWER

from SPIDER-MAN: INTO THE SPIDER-VERSE

TENOR SAX

Words and Music by AUSTIN RICHARD POST,
CARL AUSTIN ROSEN, KHALIF BROWN,
CARTER LANG, LOUIS BELL
and BILLY WALSH

Copyright © 2018 SONGS OF UNIVERSAL, INC., POSTY PUBLISHING, ELECTRIC FEEL MUSIC, WARNER-TAMERLANE PUBLISHING CORP.,
KHALIF BROWN BMI PUB DESIGNEE, EARDRUMMERS ENTERTAINMENT LLC, WC MUSIC CORP., CARTER LANG PUB DESIGNEE, ZUMA TUNA LLC,
EMI APRIL MUSIC INC., NYANKINGMUSIC, WMMW PUBLISHING, TWENTY FIFTEEN BOULEVARD MUSIC INC. and TWENTY FIFTEEN AVENUE MUSIC INC.
All Rights for POSTY PUBLISHING and ELECTRIC FEEL MUSIC Administered by SONGS OF UNIVERSAL, INC.
All Rights for KHALIF BROWN BMI PUB DESIGNEE and EARDRUMMERS ENTERTAINMENT LLC Administered by WARNER-TAMERLANE PUBLISHING CORP.
All Rights for CARTER LANG PUB DESIGNEE and ZUMA TUNA LLC Administered by WC MUSIC CORP.
All Rights for EMI APRIL MUSIC INC., NYANKINGMUSIC, WMMW PUBLISHING, TWENTY FIFTEEN BOULEVARD MUSIC INC.
and TWENTY FIFTEEN AVENUE MUSIC INC. Administered by SONY/ATV MUSIC PUBLISHING LLC, 424 Church Street, Suite 1200, Nashville, TN 37219
All Rights Reserved   Used by Permission

WORK

TENOR SAX

Words and Music by ROBYN FENTY,
JAHRON BRATHWAITE, ALLEN RITTER,
AUBREY GRAHAM, MATTHEW SAMUELS,
MONTE S. MOIR and RICHARD STEPHENSON

Moderately

© 2015, 2016 MONICA FENTY MUSIC PUBLISHING, WC MUSIC CORP., SONY/ATV MUSIC PUBLISHING LLC, EMI APRIL MUSIC INC., RITTER BOY, SANDRA GALE,
1DAMENTIONAL PUBLISHING LLC, NEW PERSPECTIVE PUBLISHING, AVANT-GARDE-MUSIC PUBLISHING, INC. and GREENSLEEVES PUBLISHING LTD.
All Rights for MONICA FENTY MUSIC PUBLISHING Administered by WARNER-TAMERLANE PUBLISHING CORP.
All Rights for SONY/ATV MUSIC PUBLISHING LLC, EMI APRIL MUSIC INC., RITTER BOY, SANDRA GALE, 1DAMENTIONWAL PUBLISHING LLC
and NEW PERSPECTIVE PUBLISHING Administered by SONY/ATV MUSIC PUBLISHING LLC, 424 Church Street, Suite 1200, Nashville, TN 37219
All Rights for AVANT-GARDE-MUSIC PUBLISHING, INC. Administered by UNIVERSAL MUSIC CORP.
All Rights Reserved   Used by Permission

To Coda ⊕

CODA

D.S. al Coda

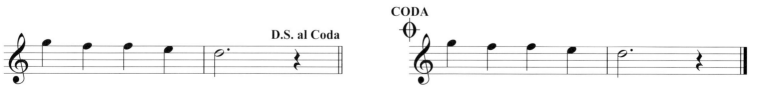

TRUTH HURTS

TENOR SAX

Words and Music by LIZZO,
ERIC FREDERIC, JESSE ST. JOHN GELLER
and STEVEN CHEUNG

© 2019 WARNER-TAMERLANE PUBLISHING CORP., MELISSA JEFFERSON PUBLISHING DESIGNEE,
SONY/ATV MUSIC PUBLISHING LLC, EMI BLACKWOOD MUSIC INC., SONGS FROM THE BOARDWALK,
FREDERIC AND RIED MUSIC, JESSE SJ MUSIC, BIG DEAL NOTES and TELE THE BUSINESS
All Rights for MELISSA JEFFERSON PUBLISHING DESIGNEE Administered by WARNER-TAMERLANE PUBLISHING CORP.
All Rights for SONY/ATV MUSIC PUBLISHING LLC, EMI BLACKWOOD MUSIC INC., SONGS FROM THE BOARDWALK, FREDERIC AND RIED MUSIC
and JESSE SJ MUSIC Administered by SONY/ATV MUSIC PUBLISHING LLC, 424 Church Street, Suite 1200, Nashville, TN 37219
International Copyright Secured   All Rights Reserved